PREFACE.

Two images of the life and the ministry of Jesus confront us to-day; the ecclesiastical image, which is the product of unsifted matter, and the critical, which is the product of matter that has passed the ordeal of the critical and historical method. A few friends of the Church in Hanover desired to acquire, in outline at least, a knowledge of this latter. This led to the preparation and finally to the publication of these lectures. The wisdom of venturing a sketch, where a complete picture was necessary, of "popularizing" sciences which were as yet hardly complete, of saying things that might perhaps create danger and unrest, may well be questioned. Such considerations led the lecturer to permit at first only a limited and manuscript impression of them. But the need of reforming and developing our traditional and ecclesiastical views is so urgent and imperative as to justify every honorable attempt directed to this end. And if the sciences of historical and critical investigation are not yet complete, the general foundation and the entire direction of the movement have been determined long ago. And if these investigations into the origins of our religion disturb and disquiet some, they emancipate and reinstate others. The knowledge that these lectures were instrumental to such ends and the fact that a mere manuscript impression called forth a public attack, led to their publication. It is to be hoped that the intention of the author will be so far respected as to restrain any one from using them for purposes of propaganda, and that his judgment regarding them shall be accepted, namely, that if they succeed in getting the readers to properly relate themselves to the subjects under discussion and to acquaint themselves more thoroughly with them, their mission will have been fulfilled.

Göttingen, February, 1902.

CONTENTS.

THE HISTORICAL SOURCES FOR THE LIFE AND MINISTRY OF JESUS.

I am to speak to you of the life and ministry of Jesus, according to the historical and scientific conception. The first question, then, is: Whence do we derive our knowledge of the person, of the ministry, and of the life of Jesus? What are the sources of the history?

Substantially the only sources are the Scriptures of the New Testament. The New Testament is not a single book; it is almost a small library of books and booklets, which were composed at different times, by different authors, and with very different contents and purposes. The Church gathered them in the course of its first centuries. It was convinced that in them it possessed products of its classical period, namely, the Apostolic age, and also trustworthy memoirs and authentic records of its origin. This collection was made not without great caution, and not without historical sense and admirable tact. It chose from a great number of less worthy and uncertain materials those which, for ethical and religious reasons, stood the highest, and which had pre-eminently the greatest claim to genuineness, that is, Apostolic or primitive origin, and to authentic narration. But in spite of this, a more searching and historical investigation could not rest satisfied with this verdict; we must revise it more thoroughly, applying to it the most modern methods of research known to historical, religious, and linguistic criticism. Accordingly the New Testament as a whole, the Gospels and the Apostolic writings, have been subjected anew, book by book, to the severest and the most scrutinizing examination. This led to many changes in our judgment. Positions which had for centuries been regarded as certain and incontestable began to shift, became precarious, and proved to be untenable or uncertain. Innumerable questions were proposed and a chaos of answers follows. Everything was in a state of fermentation. Gradually, however, order and peace were again restored. Results of an assured character were brought to light, and a firm foundation was disclosed for further building. But amid all the storms of critical discussion, the four great epistles of Paul, Galatians, I and II Corinthians, and Romans, proved to be indisputable. Scientific criticism today is agreed to all intents and purposes upon the question of the integrity of these epistles. They purport to be and stand forth as the work of the Apostle; a man who was a member of the Apostolic circle, and who wrote them about twenty years after the Master's death.

Certainly these letters do not signify much for our present purpose. They are far from being descriptions of the life and the ministry of Jesus; they are pamphlets written for other purposes, filled with instructions, consolations, admonitions, and personal affairs. The references which they make to the life, the words, and the actions of Jesus are merely incidental; but they are of great value for historical science. They give with certainty the frame work and the most general features of the life and ministry of Jesus, they give us the deepest foundation for the historic image of the Savior.

These four letters being genuine—and they are so—the following facts are incontestable: there lived at one time a person by the name of Jesus, who, unquestionably possessed the highest power and the supremest worth, and who left a most lasting impression upon a community of disciples. We know in detail, that he was a public teacher and an active preacher; that he gathered twelve "disciples" about him; that out of his ministry there went forth a community of adherents which differed from Judaism; that he claimed to be the Messiah; that he succumbed to and was crucified by the hatred of the rulers of his people and by the treachery of one of his disciples; that his followers believed that he had come forth from the dead and that he would return in the immediate future. Some of his words are cited and it is narrated that, prior to his death, he had celebrated with his followers what is known as the Lord's Supper. And what is of the greatest significance of all, these Pauline letters give expression to a piety of a unique warmth, sincerity, and power, a piety, which compared with Judaism bespeaks most unquestionably a higher grade of religion, and which, disengaged from its theological, speculative, and special Pauline setting, can certainly be traced back to the essential content and character of the preaching and the new piety of Jesus himself. These Pauline data are, as stated, only very general and very few; but they suffice to give us a detailed image of the person of Jesus and of his ministry. But to have these critically assured renders them invaluable; they give a general rule by which to guide further investigation, and they deliver us at once from all the speculations and phantasies of those who attempt to dissolve the entire life-image of Jesus into vague legends, Indo-Brahmanic, Buddhistic and the like.

For the details of this picture, we must depend wholly on the first four books of the New Testament, the Gospels. But it is a pity that here we are not on such secure ground as in the four great Pauline letters. It is only with great labor and step by step that investigation proceeds here, and separates by slow work the reliable and authentic narrative from the unreliable and the unauthentic, the historic from the unhistoric. To trace this process here in all its several steps is impossible. But we wish to sketch in general outline at least, this laborious restoration of historic truth.

First, we recognize discrepancies in the narration and general character of the several Gospels, and we ask where clear, original, historic tradition is to be found, and where not. A most remarkable contrast exists between the first three Gospels on the one side, and the Gospel of John on the other. Even Matthew, Mark, and Luke differ from one another in many respects, although manifesting a striking agreement in essentials. The historical material as a whole, the capital stock, so to speak, is alike in the three. The thread of the narrative as well as the entire sketch of the life of Jesus is also alike in them; it is simple, naively childlike, without reflection, without art, and without any design. The entire horizon, the general religious conceptions, and the theological apparatus, so to speak, are also alike.

But when we pass to the Fourth Gospel all this undergoes a remarkable change. The difference between the discourses in the Synoptics and the discourses in the Fourth Gospel manifests itself everywhere. The Synoptics are characterized by short, pithy, and precise expressions, reaching the hearts and consciences of the hearers and leaving an indelible impression upon them; or by picturesque, animating parables, incomparable for their simplicity and directness. John is altogether different: the speeches are long, solemn, deep, difficult, abstract, ofttimes undecided, studiedly ambiguqus by reason of the profundity of expression, poor in images, partial to allegories, but seldom forming genuinely plastic parables. The expression on the whole is more like that of a solemn school-master than that of a great and irresistible national preacher. Moreover, the change in the theology of the authors strikes one immediately. The Synoptics are naively and popularly simple; the Gospel of John emulates the higher speculation. The author of the Fourth Gospel is acquainted with the philosophy of his time. His Christianity has not, for this reason, become a philosophy, but it is no longer expounded with the simplicity characteristic of its three predecessors; it appears rather in the garb of philosophic expression. The beginning of his Gospel shows us this at once by its application of the leading concept of the Alexandrian philosophy to the person of Christ; the concept of the "Logos," the Eternal Word, that is, the reason dwelling within God, which was before all time, and by which all things were made. The author's aim was to make it intelligible to his age that God had revealed himself in Jesus; and it was on this view as a foundation, that he built his Gospel. Furthermore, the image of the Christ life in the Fourth Gospel differs greatly from that of the Synoptics. We have already suggested that he was more solemnly pathetic here than elsewhere; we must now add that the clear and most decisive individuality of Jesus, with its definite temperament and nature, is hardly present in the Fourth Gospel; the *idea* dominates the whole. It is true of the personality of Jesus as of the historic matter in general, that the narrative, which in the Synoptics is so vivid and animating as to bring us the very atmosphere and coloring of the historical situation, serves here simply to fill in the frame work of thought.

It is freely handled, shifted, and even inverted; its chief aim is to become a transparent veil for a profound idea. Closely connected with this is the way in which this Gospel lifts the form of Jesus wholly into the sphere of the miraculous and the absolutely superhuman. Certainly this tendency amply and powerfully attests its presence in the Synoptics, but there we can trace its progress. Its historical roots ever look out upon us, and the form of the miracle worker has not been lifted, for so long a time, so completely into the realms of the supernatural. His miracle-working power meets difficulties, submits to necessary conditions, and there are instances where he is unable to perform the miracle. He is not able to do all things; he is neither all-powerful nor all-knowing. He confesses his ignorance of the times of the kingdom; and he confesses it peacefully, calling forth no surprise on the part of his disciples, because on the whole he remains within the confines of the human and so to speak of the human faculty. It is otherwise in the Fourth Gospel; the Logos background on which the picture of the Christ is sketched gleams through everywhere. He is above all opposition and conditions here; he sees through men and things without difficulty. He undertakes exceptional things without any trouble, changes

water into wine, and awakens Lazarus who had
already been three days in the grave and with
whom, therefore, the process of decomposition
had already begun.

Thus and in various other ways, the
Fourth Gospel differs from the Synoptics.
And more than this the whole argument
serves to show that the Synoptic accounts
are, for the most part, very close to historical
reality, whereas the Gospel of John is very remote from it. The aim of the historical portion
is to be the allegory of the idea. Certainly
these ideas belong to the highest and the most
significant in the New Testament. And indeed
they are genuine Christian treasures, spirit of
the spirit of the Christ. Moreover this accounts
for the special value set upon the Fourth Gospel by the Church. For this reason also it
will ever continue as one of the Church's eternal and invaluable possessions. But it is evident that, when we seek after reliable sources
for the history of Jesus, this Gospel is to be
excluded for the same reason, and that we are
first of all to confine ourselves rather exclusively to the Synoptics. Here too we get in
abundance what is missing in the Gospel of
John: plain historical reminiscence. It is almost astonishing how clear and how true the
historical situation has been preserved; indi-

vidual things, attendant circumstances, and
even small details are brought to our notice,
which never could have been invented. Those
factors had long been active here to which, in
particular, D. F. Strauss directed the attention of the world; the unconscious and unde-
signed invention and unfolding of the legend,
the tendency to exaggeration and development
into the miraculous, the injection of Old Testament and Judaic representations and ideals, according to which the narrative imperceptibly
formed itself. Indeed entire portions of the
Synoptics themselves are legendary, and there
is many a real and historic event touched by
the same tendency. But the authenticity of
large portions of them is above suspicion. And
with a little trouble, the historically and theo-
logically disciplined critic—although not every
amateur—can separate (not perhaps in all cases
with absolute certainty) the historic from the
unhistoric or the half-historic. And this is true
in ever-widening certainty where the cases are
most important and decisive and where the
image of Jesus and his ministry as a whole are
concerned.

Having excluded the Fourth Gospel as a
source of history, criticism proceeds to separate
the reliable from the less reliable within the
Synoptics. Even an amateur may with some

attention distinguish Mark as the Synoptic Gospel which stands nearest the reality of history. As the Synoptics are simpler than John, so the Gospel of Mark is simpler than its companions, Matthew and Luke. Where Mark is clear, direct, and simple, evincing traces of the historical situation, Matthew and Luke treating the same matter are circuitous, embodying adapted traditions, scribal changes, condensation and simplifications. Furthermore, the tendency to the miraculous is on the increase from Mark to Matthew and Luke. We might have expected that the nearer the narrative to the source itself the less would be this tendency; whereas the more remote, the greater it would be. And this corresponds with the conditions in Mark, Matthew, and Luke. As a slight but signal instance of this, examine the accounts of the baptism and the anointing of Jesus by the Holy Ghost. Mark represents it with tolerable clearness as an inner "visionary" experience of Jesus. It says, "he *saw* the heavens open." Matthew however has already externalized the event. He describes it thus, "And lo the heavens *were opened.*" Not satisfied with saying that the Spirit of God descended in the form of a dove, Luke assures us that "the Holy Spirit descended in *bodily* form." The very same tendency reveals itself largely in the gradual growth of the legendary matter at the commencement and at the close of the three Gospels in the narratives of the birth and the resurrection. Mark's account of this event at the close of his Gospel, is very short: the weeping women at the tomb were commanded by an angel to go to Galilee, where they should see the risen one. Matthew already shows an extended growth of the miraculous element. It is related that the angel descended, rolled away the stone, sat thereon, and that "his countenance was like lightning, and his raiment white as snow." Already the disciples themselves as well as the women go to the grave, see the risen one, and receive instructions from him to go to Galilee. It is also added that he appeared to them there. Luke tells us that there were two angels at the grave, that Jesus appeared to the assembly within closed doors, that he permitted himself to be touched, and that he ate in their presence. Luke adds the ascension also to this account of the crucifixion. The same thing is true of the legendary birth stories and the introductory history. Luke gives us the legend in its more developed form; Matthew in a less developed form; whereas Mark shows no traces of it.

The Gospel according to Mark thus evinces itself from every standpoint to be the oldest and the first Gospel. And not only this; the two other Gospels, Matthew and Luke are not only younger than Mark and dependent upon it in their narration, but they include it within their own pages. This can be easily shown with regard to Matthew. We can duplicate entire passages in Matthew which have been taken almost literally from Mark. Truly these portions have been redacted, slightly changed and somewhat impaired by being worked over with other traditional matter; but we can easily detect Mark as one source of Matthew.

If we thus disengage the Gospel of Mark from Matthew, a second surprising and beautiful result comes to light. What remains of Matthew—that is, apart from the birth and resurrection narratives, which do not belong to it—forms a second ancient source, itself a small book. This is probably still older than Mark, and while Mark gives itself chiefly to the narration of events, it devotes itself almost entirely to the "Sayings of the Lord," parables, sentences and longer expressions joined together like a necklace of pearls, of which the Sermon on the Mount is an example. No doubt we have here preserved the most genuine portion of all the trustworthy tradition, which was doubtless once a little book by itself. Some later person interwove it with the Gospel of Mark, which had been written in the meanwhile, adding also the legends which had become public property, and thus Matthew was written.

After Matthew, Luke was written. The first verse of this Gospel attests the lateness of its composition. The time of the "original eye-witnesses" had long passed away. It drew its materials from tradition, oral and written. Legendary matter has a large place in its pages. Already individual "apocryphal" traits manifest themselves. Still this ranks in feeling with the best of traditions. Its chief sources are Mark and the Lord's Sayings. And there is much matter that streams in from other sides, matter which is easily recognized as true gold; as, for instance, the group of beautiful parables peculiar to Luke.

A SKETCH OF THE LIFE AND MINISTRY OF JESUS.

Having thus properly although meagerly related ourselves to the "sources of the history" of Jesus, we are now prepared to trace their image of His Life and His Ministry.

*   *

*

The Gospel of Mark begins very plainly with the superscription: "Beginning of the Gospel of Jesus Christ," and forthwith proceeds to describe the appearance of John the Baptist and the baptism of Jesus in the Jordan. This indeed is the commencement of the reliable history of Jesus. The portions of Matthew and Luke, which treat of the preceding years, the years covering the prenatal, the natal, and the immediately postnatal circumstances, belong, according to the historical and critical method, to the beautiful frame work with which legend is accustomed to embellish historical reality.*

The preliminary history is full of the most tender and beautiful legends: the sending of the archangel, "the angelic greeting," the journey to Bethlehem, the shepherds in the field, the angel voices proclaiming "Fear not!" and "Glory to God in the highest!" the babe in the manger, the allegiance of the three wise men from the East, the leading of the star as of some heavenly guide that "went before them, till it came and stood over where the young child was," the greeting given to the new-born child by Simeon and Anna in the temple, Mary's visit to Elizabeth, Herod's anger, and the flight to Egypt. Now this is poetic legend from beginning to end, but even as such it towers far above the confused and senseless fables of later apocryphal evangelical literature and forms an excellent frame work to the historical image of

---

*"The senseless confusion of 'legend' with 'lying' has caused good people to hesitate to concede that there are legends in the Old Testament. But legends are not lies; on the contrary, they are a particular form of poetry........ ..
Now, since legend and history are very different in both origin and nature, there are many criteria by which they may be distinguished. One of the chief points of difference is that legend is chiefly oral tradition, while history is usually found in written form; this is inherent in the nature of the two species, legend being the tradition of those who are not in the habit of writing, while history, which is a sort of scientific activity, presupposes writing." See pages 3 and 4 of Dr. Hermann Gunkel's *Legends of Genesis*, translated by Dr. Carruth (Chicago Open Court Pub. Co., 1901)—Trans.

the Christ. And no one will permit himself, or willingly be the cause of permitting others, to be deprived of hearing again and again these beautiful narratives of the Advent and Christmastide. But this does not remove the duty of distinguishing between legend and history, and of teaching others who are entrusted to us to make this distinction. The task may appear a difficult one, but it is unavoidable and it is possible. A very large circle of readers have already grasped the distinction between the authority and the worth of the Scriptures in the religious and the ethical realm and the same authority in the physical and geographical realm. The geocentric character of much of our Biblical teaching has not discredited them as the instruments of spiritual culture. The discernment of the distinction between ''holy saga'' and ''holy history'' in Bible story is destined to run a similar course. And if this is permitted to come to pass at the proper time, it will not disturb the high position which these writings hold at present; indeed it will in many instances establish or, we may say, re-establish faith. It is inevitable that the concepts ''holy saga'' and ''holy history,'' which are recognized today in all up-to-date theology, should also enter into the domain of religious instruction.

But it may be asked: will the recognition of the introductory part of the life as legendary destroy any of the significance of the Christmas festival? By no means. Mature Christians already realize that the angel voices and the frame work of miracle are not the chief things; they know that these are mere decorations. The holiday really celebrates the birth of Christ; and this will remain equally sacred and equally worthy of celebration even after this distinction has been generally accepted; it will remain just as if no legend had ever gathered about the original fact.

That one is really occupied with legends and not with history in this part of the story is evident at once to all who have any skill in distinguishing between the history of religion and the formation of legend. But even the remaining parts of the New Testament do not seem to regard the birth stories as genuine history; Paul knows nothing of them, nor does Mark pay any attention to them. The silence of the Johannean Gospel is instructive on these matters; the more so when we remember that Matthew and Luke had been completed a long time before and had become the common possession of a large circle, and that the dogma of the virgin birth was already in general favor. Now this Gospel grasps at the highest

conceptions and expressions, at the conception
of the incarnation of the Eternal Logos, to illustrate and to lay firmly the foundation of the
uniqueness and the significance of Jesus; and
yet it makes no reference to the virgin birth
nor to any other singularity of the child legend.
This looks like a deliberate rejection of these
conceptions, which he perhaps must have
thought all too primitive and anthropomorphic
to explain his Logos Christ.

Properly to appreciate this subject one can
hardly do better than to follow the gradual
growth of the legendary matter from Matthew
to Luke. Matthew represents the legend in
the stage of formation, the simpler form; nothing more than that Joseph is told in a dream
that the child to be born was of the Holy Ghost.
Luke gives a more developed account; relates
the sending of the angel Gabriel to the virgin,
her meekness, and their conversation. One can
almost see the legend growing as it passes from
mouth to mouth; and this was not confined to
the introductory history of the Messiah alone,
it was also applied to the early history of John
the Baptist. The parallel is almost complete,
covering the pre-natal visitation and the signs
that followed it. But the strongest New Testament proof of the legendary character of the
birth narrative is the conduct of the mother and

the relatives of Jesus at his public appearance. They do not understand him; they know nothing of his higher nature; they hinder him, continue incredulous, and wish him to return home even after he has commenced his work. They are not amenable to his teaching, proclaiming him to be beside himself. But Jesus renounces them, proclaiming his followers to be his brethren. This would have been altogether impossible, if only a part of the introductory history had really happened.

For historical and critical science, Jesus is the son of Joseph. He was known by this name in Nazareth, and it was the original conception of him. This is almost naively sét forth in the two genealogies, purporting to be the proof of his Davidic descent. But both registers trace the line to Joseph; a fact which clearly presupposes Jesus to be the son of Joseph. Indeed it was conjectured a long time ago that the conclusion of the register must have read, "But Joseph begat Jesus." And this conjecture received a very surprising ratification a few years ago, when a Syrian Gospel manuscript, the oldest extant, was discovered in the cloister of Catherine on Sinai. Now, according to this text, the reading in Matthew i. 16, is not what we have today; the original form one can plainly detect to be: "But Joseph begat Jesus."*

The question, then, today, concerning the narrative of the birth is not: "Is it history or legend?" but "What are the motives that led to the formation of the legend?" The history of religion will yet have to clear up this subject. Meanwhile we may indicate the answer in the light of present thought. It is a common religious phenomenon that the founder of a religious community is exempted more and more by the faith of his followers from the natural course of things, and that his appearance, in particular, is attributed to superhuman factors. Thus there are parallels elsewhere to the birth legends of Jesus; the cases for instance of Zoroaster and Plato. The most signal, however, is

*In his *History of the Christian Church*, George Park Fisher, D. D., LL.D., at one time Titus Street Professor of Ecclesiastical History in Yale University, makes the following remarks concerning the doctrine of the immaculate conception. "In the twelfth century the doctrine of the Virgin's immaculate conception was broached. This view was embraced by the Franciscans, who were specially zealous in rendering honor to Mary. It was rejected by the Dominicans, and formed a standing subject of controversy down to a recent date." Page 226.

Writing of Pius IX, in connection with this doctrine, he says: "In 1854, he gathered a large company of ecclesiastics at Rome, and promulgated on his own personal responsibility, without the concurrence of any council, the dogma of the immaculate conception of the Virgin. He thus assumed to decide authoritatively a question which the doctors of the Church had long debated, and on which they are not yet agreed." Page 537.—Trans.

that of Buddha. He also had no human father;
was born amid signs and wonders; his birth
was celebrated by heavenly bands; and soon
after his birth, he was recognized by priests
and seers as the coming light. The parallel is
very striking. It was thought that the re-
semblances were due to borrowing, but this is
a mistake for no trace of any dependency has
ever been found. On the contrary, legends of
a like character have sprung up in so many different places as to indicate laws and motives
common to them all. But furthermore, in ad-
dition to what it has in common with phenomena of its class, there are factors in the Christian legend, which help to determine its present form. Strauss was correct here. The Old
Testament patriarchal and prophetic narratives and the current Judaic representations of
the Messiah, which were powerful factors in
the Christian community, were great forces in
the formation of the legend. The dreams, the
visions, the angelic predictions, took their rise
in this way. Both Isaac and Jacob were sons
of the promise and the peculiar power of God.
Likewise Samuel. Indeed since the time of
Jeremiah, it was the general view that the mes-
sengers of God were chosen and predestined
by him from the mother's womb. How much
more must this have been the case with the

Messiah? He was regarded as a semi-super-natural being, and it was the most natural thing in the world to assume that his advent would not conform to the methods of nature. Add to this that Isaiah vii. 14, was read ''Behold a virgin shall conceive, and bear a son.'' Indeed, Isaiah was not thinking of the Messiah in this passage, but it was referred to him. Furthermore the original is not ''virgin,'' but ''woman.'' But the Greek translation and the current explanation read ''virgin,'' as we see in Matthew i. 23. Here, undoubtedly, under the influence of this misunderstood passage of Isaiah, we discover the main origin of the doctrine of the virgin birth. Apart from this, the legend would perhaps have entered the same pathway as did that of John at a later date.

We know nothing of the history of Jesus before his public appearance save the temple incident of his twelfth year, and criticism has at times contested even this, but without sufficient reason. The incident itself is not necessarily miraculous or legendary. The boy of twelve in the orient is mature, and it is not to be wondered at that his future religious genius should thus early and prophetically become manifest. We know only the following facts about his early years: that he was the son of plain parents; that he sprang from Nazareth, a small Galilean mountain village, known to this day midway between the Galilean sea and the gulf of Haifa; that he received neither a Grecian nor indeed a Rabbinical culture,—nothing save the plain "religious instruction" from the holy books of his people; but that he learned to read these with a clearer and deeper appreciation than the scholars and the religious specialists of his time. He required a long period for his mental development, for the maturing of his unique religious character, and for the awakening of the knowledge of his higher mission. He entered upon his ministry in his thirtieth year, a ripe age for the rapidly developing oriental, but he soon manifested the greatest power, leaving behind him the greatest effects. He was at first far from entertaining the project of a world mission or an eternal mission. It was merely a local and a temporary movement like the movement of the Baptist, which certainly was the occasion of the appearance of Jesus.

What then was the design of the Baptist? It was certainly something completely local and temporary. The Jewish people had been subject for centuries to the oppression of changing dynasties. But the stronger the oppression the more intense grew the longing for the interposition of God. All the ancient promises of the prophecies of the past concerning the final magnificence of Judah and Jerusalem and concerning the overthrow of the enemy blazed up again. These prophecies were indeed originally directed against Assyria and Babylon; but they were applied spontaneously to the new condition of things; and new promises that God would in the near future take compassion upon his people were added to them. All these hopes, wishes and dreams were gathered up into the thought of the "kingdom of God," or "the kingdom of heaven," which was supposed to be at the door and which was to be realized in splendor and supernatural glory in Judah. Imagination ran riot with this thought; and its picture which continued to grow in color and supernatural proportions, was handed on from generation to generation, now as an object of consolation and now as an object of hope. A complete and unique literature sprang up called "The Revelations," depicting the coming kingdom in visions, images and allegories, sometimes highly poetic and sometimes very prosaic. But with this thought of the kingdom of God, the ancient Messianic representation broke out powerfully again. Isaiah had prophesied that, after the downfall and the destruction of the nation and the Davidic kingdom, this latter would be re-established, and that a God-gifted scion would spring from its root as a hero and a ruler to build anew the Jewish nation. This prophecy had not been fulfilled, the surviving family had not accomplished what was hoped of it, and the dynasty itself had sunk into insignificance. But the hope for the "anointed," the expected hero, continued from generation to generation. It grew to be at once a theological concept and a favorite subject of the artistic fancy. The image broke away entirely from its historic, Isaianic, and fundamental thought, assuming fantastic and superhuman features.

But this hope of a coming kingdom did not exhaust itself in the production of mere books and pious wishes. It broke out into turbulent convulsions and movements against compulsory power, it brought forth Pseudo-Messiahs, and it won for itself heralds and prophets. John was one of these. He also announced that "the kingdom was at hand," that "the axe is laid unto the root of the trees," and with expectant eyes, he looked for "him that cometh after me"; but the announcement took a different character with him. He announced the coming of the kingdom, but did not for this reason urge the people "to take up arms," as the agitators and reformers generally had done, but urged them to repentance. For him the kingdom of God was to be realized not bv the power of man, but by the miraculous interposition of God. He called men to complete resignation and absolute obedience to God. The old prophetic idea awoke within him: "God comes only to a people of pure hands and pure heart. Only those of a pure heart enter this kingdom."

Breaking away thus from the zealots, the theocratic agitators, the fanatics, and the political aspirants, he became a great preacher of righteousness. The goal of all his activity was repentance from sin, complete subjection to the divine law, severe discipline, and fasting, and he baptized them in the Jordan as a sign of cleansing and purification. He wielded an immense power over his contemporaries. Multitudes streamed to hear him, and a band of disciples formed about him. Many carried the announcement of the approaching kingdom and the need of repentance from him to their own homes and circles.

Now Jesus also came at first as one of this class and being taken up by the call and the preaching of John, he submitted to baptism and departed home to deliver, as it seems, the same message: "Repent for the kingdom of heaven is at hand." But it soon became evident that he was greater than John, and that he had a better Gospel for his people. But we shall treat of this hereafter. We shall first of all follow the sketch of his life to the end.

Jesus received his call, his higher mission, in an event, at the baptism. According to Matthew and Luke this was external; according to Mark, which gives the simpler and the more intelligible account, it was internal. It happened to him as to the great prophets of Israel, an Isaiah or a Jeremiah. Isaiah was not a self-constituted prophet and messenger of God. He was called and almost driven against his will to the thorny vocation of a prophet by a spiritual experience, the power and grandeur of which is still felt in the mere narrative. In this vision he saw God in his temple sitting upon a high throne, heard his voice and the fearful message which he was to bring to Jehovah's people. It was thus that Jesus saw the heavens opened and received the words which made him what he was at the opening of his ministry. What kind of experience was this? We read of visions, "of visual and auditory hallucinations," and we forthwith construct some plausible psychological explanation of them: "Powerful excitement of the feelings, plastic fancy, excessive nervousness." But do these uncover the real secret of the matter? Do they explain the immediate certainty of all prophetic consciousness? The bed-rock certainty which is part of the endowment, and which gives its bearers iron foreheads against worlds of oppositions, attacks, and impossibilities? A certainty that errs not for a moment, even where all seems to break up and to be in vain; not where disciples prove treacherous; not indeed in the bloody sweat of Gethsemane? A purely positivistic method of reading history may satisfy itself with such explanations; but one who is not foresworn will think otherwise. He will not believe that the heavens opened and that the spirit descended in the form of a dove, or that Jehovah appeared bodily with a train of seraphs. He will be convinced that all this is the objectivization of an unnameable inner experience, with all the above mentioned conceptions even to "hallucination" playing their part. But he will also grant to this subjective experience its mystery and its reality.

Before Jesus began his ministry "he was led by the Spirit into the wilderness to be tempted of the devil." There is no mountain from which one can see "all the kingdoms of this world and their glory," nor is it thinkable that the young Nazarene was carried through the air and placed upon a pinnacle of the temple. But one can easily think and understand that before entering upon his work, Jesus would betake himself, for personal reasons, to prayer and fasting in the wilderness—as a Paul and an Elias did—and that, in this loneliness, he would have to choose between the popular and the political idea of the Messiah, which he must have known, and the spiritual and self-denying ideal, which he carried in his own heart. He was passing through a great struggle: Should he choose the way of the poor preacher and fisher of men, or should he choose the way of the enthusiast, the way of the national hero? This temptation could not be avoided. It was latent in the spirit and the consciousness of the age. Jesus conquered. What Philippians ii. 5-7, affirms respecting the pre-existent Christ, proved to be true respecting the Christ of history: he chose the way of humility rather than the way of the "robber."

He began his ministry on the shore of the Galilean sea. Its leading features are presented to us in the Gospels. He preached in the synagogues, in the homes of his friends, on all kinds of occasion, at the table, under the free heavens, now here and now there. His calling was especially extended by the mysterious gift of healing that had been awakened within him.

What was this mysterious power? We have already seen that the Jesus of the *Synoptics* is not the absolute wonder worker that he seems sometimes to be in John or in the traditional view. But even in those parts of the Gospels which have sustained the severest criticism, he stands forth possessing something inexplicable. This is true of his gift of healing. The narratives of his healing ministry evince such verity as to exclude even the thought of a legendary origin. Examine, for instance, the almost business like account of the healing of Peter's wife's mother, Mark i. 29-31, or the realistic account of the man with the palsy, or the cases of the nobleman of Capernaum and the Canaanitish woman. That wonderful dialectic between Jesus and the woman in which he at first opposes her, but then grants her the blessing, is worth attending to. Poetic legend does not grow in this way. Add to this that we meet like phenomena within the first Christian communities. Were we inclined to attack the Gospel narratives of the healing practised by Jesus we could not well deny the same phenomena in Corinth, in Galatia, and in Rome; phenomena which happened in the broadest light of history and of historical attestation. The original community and Paul were clearly convinced that they possessed the *Charismata,* the "gifts," among themselves. A formal catalogue of them is given in 1 Cor. xii. 4-11: the gift of tongues, the gift of prophetic power (clairvoyance), the gift of healing and of mighty deeds and also other psychical powers. But one may well remember that he added something that has greater worth than all of these gifts, namely, the simple Christian virtues, faith, love, and hope, and that the greatest of these is love. But this evidently presupposed the reality and the presence of the afore-mentioned gifts. He possessed them himself, and exercised them repeatedly. Indeed, they appeared in all the communities. One may go further, there is certain historical evidence that these very *"gifts"* existed far beyond the Apostolic age. And there is similar evidence that an analagous class of gifts were found scattered in circles not Christian. The question may be asked: will this mysterious realm be open to us again? To return a negative answer simply because it does not accord with our ideas of "the course of nature" would be un-historic. A fair and candid reading of the critically sifted portions of the Gospels cannot but strengthen the impression that Jesus possessed this power or these powers in an unusual degree. Moreover our earlier studies of the peculiar parts and "natural endowments" of the great Old Testament prophets, have already given us a key, so to speak, to this matter. They were not omniscient; they did not possess the ability to forecast the future for centuries; but they did possess, in many instances, a peculiar presentiment and divination of menacing events of an extraordinary character, events too that soon befell them. This gift then appears to us, not as "supernatural" and miraculous in the ancient sense of that term, that is, as something completely outside of the analogy of current events; on the contrary, we find illustrations of this extraordinary character in the phenomena of clairvoyance, farsightedness, the faculty of divination of particularly gifted natures, and second sight and the like.

Perhaps Christ's gift of healing which seems so mysterious to us, was "only" a development of capabilities slumbering in human nature in general. The prime instance of the effective influence of a psychical agent upon a physical reality, is the power of the will to move the body: a spiritual cause producing a mechanical result. This is an absolute mystery; and were it not so common it would still be recognized as such. But who will undertake to exhaust *a priori* the possibilities of such a realm? Who will define what a will may accomplish in an unmediated ministry, a will in full control of its powers and in deepest sympathy with God? In more recent times, people have frequently endeavored to institute a parallel between the miracles of Jesus and the newly discovered hypnotic and telepathic methods and the like. And

why should we not accept it, if we add that the
works of Jesus extend far beyond the sphere
of our knowledge, and that they always emanate
from the consciousness of his mission, and that
whenever they incline to the extraordinary they
do so by reason of his ethical and religious consciousness and his continued dependence upon
God? And, certainly, if he was capable of such
extraordinary things, the tendency to exaggeration and invention would instantly set in, and
a wise caution respecting the narrative of the
miracles would not only be in place, but absolutely necessary. That Jesus could do wonders
is not sufficient reason for accepting everything
accredited to him by tradition. The reanima-
tion of Lazarus, and the turning of water into
wine depart very widely from that which is con-
ceivably and historically acceptable, both cases
in the Gospel of John. Even the Synoptics contain enough that outrun all conceptual possi-
bility, such as walking upon the sea, and the
feeding of the five thousand with five loaves and
two fishes. Eliminate miracles of this type,
and those left within the Synoptics would belong almost entirely to the cases of healing,
many of which are of the most astonishing character. The Synoptics, indeed, contain the narratives of two reanimations, the little daughter
of Jairus and the son of the widow of Nain.

Criticism is inclined to turn away from these, but it must always be remembered that these narratives differ essentially from that of Lazarus given in John. The little daughter of Jairus had not been three days in the grave, as Lazarus had been, she had only just lost consciousness. Where lies the boundary which divides complete death from the last and perhaps unconscious spark of life? Had he who possessed power to compose a troubled and deranged consciousness the power to halt a spirit upon the boundary line or mayhap to recall the same into the already deserted body? The narrative is strikingly concrete at this point. Even the Aramaic words, the very sounds which he used to awaken the child, are kept for us: "Talitha Cumi." All theatrical pomp which might have accompanied a public exhibition is absent. Of the disciples only the most trustworthy are admitted, and the thing concludes with the commonplace injunction that the child be given something to eat and that there be no further mention of the event. Let any one compare the case of Lazarus with this. Everything is so arranged as to create an impression. The solemn deed is done before all people. A prayer, which is an appeal to those present, accompanies the deed. The whole thing is done "because of the people." Such an account may be a product of art, hardly of life. The accounts of Mark are of a different character. A considerate criticism will suspend its judgment.

The multitude gradually approached the new prophet. He led them to the mountain or to the sea shore, seating himself at times in a boat close by. Out of the multitudes a small community formed itself, and out of this community a band of twelve disciples, called to be his immediate followers. These "followed after him" from place to place, as did the followers of other masters; as the prophets and their scholars, and the rabbis and their adherents. His calling led him out beyond the boundaries of Galilee into Judea, into the East of the land watered by the Jordan, and even into Syro-Phoenicia. Meanwhile his following kept growing; thousands accompanied him. Then the joyful hope of perhaps winning the entire nation grew within him; the mission of the twelve was directed to this end. We know the injunctions that he gave them for their first missionary journey. The impressive scene of their return is also depicted for us, and the result of their labor. We are further told of the great joy of Jesus, a joy which broke out into open thanksgiving to the Father. This is related so plainly and so truthfully that one cannot help feeling its dewy freshness.

But while his ministry kept growing, opposition and enmity sprang up, and the catastrophe slowly cast its shadows before it. He preached new and unheard of things; things that had reference to the law, to the sabbaths, to fastings, to Levitical purity and impurity, to righteousness and genuine piety, to the validity of current views, customs, and holy usages. He called forth increasingly the resistance and the opposition of the conservative parties, especially the scribes and the pharisees. Many a hope was blasted. Disillusionment, lukewarmness, and withdrawal became more frequent. The cities where he had done his greatest and most impressive works, the cities which he had called "his own," became listless and reactionary. He was constrained to proclaim his woes over Chorazin and Bethsaida. His feeling is revealed in the parable of the sower, that only a few bring forth fruit. The seed of the word fares variously; it falls upon the wayside, amid thorns and upon stony ground.

At this time and perhaps closely connected with it, a spirit of unrest took possession of him. Leaving Capernaum and the lake and continuing his journey as far as Syro-Phoenicia, he then returned and wandered about the same spot. A great resolution formed and matured itself in the depth of his soul. He must bring to a decision the whole question between God and this people. The nature of the situation forced him to this; the stagnant, the stationary and, in most cases, the reactionary character of the work rendered it imperative. Was the work already begun to be frittered away and to come to naught? The people must be compelled to accept or reject the message in accepting or rejecting the messenger. But this alternative must be brought to a head only in the center of the nation, in Jerusalem.

He determined to go up with his followers to Judea and to Jerusalem, and in a solemn manner to declare himself the Messiah of the nation, thus compelling them to receive or reject him. This was certainly an unprecedented undertaking. The terrible issue, the catastrophe, was all but a certainty. Knowing well the extreme hatred of the Jews, he also knew Jerusalem as the prophet-slaying city. He divined the result, and told his disciples that the Son of man should be taken, and that he should be delivered into the hands of the heathen, that is, to the Roman power. His soul was in great anguish yet he went up into the city. He went up not as a fanatic, but as a man under a great moral restraint; he went up to fulfil a great moral duty. He was following the moral logic of the situation, and if his outlook had been still worse he would undoubtedly have met the consequences of his ministry. And when out of pure sympathy Peter undertook to advise a change, he answered him with the sharp, cutting words: "Get thee behind me, Satan, for thou art an hindrance to me." Here he recognized the tempter's voice and conducted himself towards him as he had done in the wilderness.

He wished to declare himself the Messiah. There was something peculiar about his Messiahship. He was the Messiah of these people in one sense, but not in another. He who realized the prophetic hope was the Messiah and was entitled to the honor, but there were two different conceptions of the Messiah in the Scriptures. According to one of these the people expected Israel and Judah to be re-established in the glory of the people of God, a thoroughly political ideal; according to the other, the people expected a religious and ethical revival of their deeper life, an enhancement and unfolding of their faith, and an extension of their knowledge of God to the heathen; a conception that corresponded to the religious and ethical ideal of the "new covenant" and one that was sustained by Jeremiah and Deutero-

Isaiah. Both conceptions had often been united, but were essentially different. Jesus was farthest removed from the political ideal, he espoused the spiritual one. He was perfectly justified in proclaiming himself the Messiah, while espousing the ethical and religious view, and he did this in a thorough manner. His new piety which consisted in faith in the "Fatherhood of God," was really the development and the fulfilment of the teachings of Jeremiah and Deutero-Isaiah; it was indeed "the new covenant." His new righteousness was really the law written in the heart, prophetically foretold by Jeremiah. Jesus felt himself called to rediscover those deeper and more spiritual realities that occupied Deutero-Isaiah. Hence he felt himself constrained by every motive, psychologic and historic, to declare himself the Messiah that "was to come." Thus he construed his doctrine of the Messiah, and it was the kind of a Messiah that the people were to receive or to reject. It was undoubtedly the greatest test to which the Jews ever were or could be subjected. To accept this Messiah was to relinquish all the current dreams and hopes of political greatness which had possessed them, and to permit the divine purpose to take its own course. It was, in a word, to be converted to the idea of

piety and morality which proclaimed itself in
Jesus.

Jesus was certain of his "Messiahship"
ever since his calling. The words "Thou art
my beloved Son," which he heard then, had the
same meaning as "Thou art my Anointed One."
Indeed the solemn title for the Messiah was
"Son of God." But thus far he had made no
claim to this position and had not entrusted
even his own disciples with this secret. Hence
his joy and, one may add, his surprise was
correspondingly greater to find this conviction
gradually and intelligently forming itself in
their minds and breaking out at last in the confession, "Thou art the Christ, the Son of the
living God." The scene is given in Matthew
xvi. 13, and occurred at the beginning of that
period of wandering, not far from Caesarea.
The confession appeared so wonderful to Jesus
that he said to Peter: "Flesh and blood hath
not revealed this to thee, but my Father which
is in heaven."

It will be remembered that up to this time
Jesus had forbidden his disciples to proclaim
his Messiahship. Henceforth it was to be different; the time of silence was gone and the
time for speaking had come. As he journeyed
to Jerusalem amid the pilgrim band, it was

known that he was the Messiah and that he would enter Jerusalem as such. His Messianic character was clearly proclaimed to all the city by the exact correspondence of his entrance to the prophetic forecast. It was Zechariah that had said of the Messianic King: "Rejoice greatly, O daughter of Zion; shout, O daughter of Jerusalem: Behold thy king cometh unto thee: he is just and having salvation; lowly and riding upon an ass and upon a colt the foal of an ass." This passage was put forth figuratively in the prophet; it was to express the peaceful and unwarlike character of him who was to come. Jesus referred it to himself and gave the people to understand that he was the promised one. He commanded two of his disciples to go to Bethphage hard by Jerusalem and bring him the colt of an ass, corresponding to the prophetic statement. Being seated upon it by his disciples, he rode into Jerusalem, his way strewn with the branches of the trees and the garments of the people, and the multitude shouting: "Hosanna, blessed is he who comes in the name of the Lord." Perceiving the import of this, the chief priests and the scribes asked him: "Hearest thou what these say?" They were anxious that he should forbid the people to call him the Messiah. But he answered: "I tell you if these should hold their peace the stones would immediately cry out." The crisis was precipitated. The morrow was to see this intensified still more, inasmuch as the new Messiah would exercise his kingly prerogative by clearing the temple of its polluters.

The issue was squarely drawn. A few days and the decision of the people for or against him would be irrevocably registered. His opponents did not yet dare him; his bold deed of cleansing the temple was allowed to go unpunished. But Jesus was not misled by this illusive condition of things; he knew that this fickle people would shout hosanna today and crucify him tomorrow, and he knew the invincible character of his enemy. Still a glimmer of hope must have struggled with the growing darkness even to the very last, for in the garden of Gethsemane he offered that most touching of prayers, "Father, if it be possible let this cup pass from me." But it became increasingly evident to him that he was to endure most bitterly, and that it was the inscrutable will of God to give up his beloved to weakness and death. Indeed this had come to him when he left Galilee. He spoke of it on the way to his disciples, and then, in Bethany, when the sisters anointed his body with costly ointment, he said "against the day of my burial has she kept this." But the clearest statement of all was made on the very last night.

As this knowledge grew within him, two other thoughts also took possession of him and filled his heart. The one was: if God hands over his servant to weakness and death, he can never be indifferent to the consequences. "The death of his saints is precious in his sight," is the testimony of the Psalms. How much more the death of Jesus? God will cause him to be honored as the seal and security of the new covenant which his servant has founded between him and his followers. He had occasionally expressed this thought before, and now again in the dark hour of his betrayal the same thought possessed him as an inspiration; and, after the type of the passover of the ancient covenant, he founded a new passover for his community, the memorial supper of his death. The second thought was: it became clear to him that he was to fall in this fight, which would carry in the common judgment of that age a condemnation of his work. But Jesus had another view of the case. His faith never wavered for a moment; indeed it grew in unprecedented strength and boldness. If God permitted his messenger to die in shame, he would also by some means or other help him to final victory.

The expressions, and the images of the book of
Daniel came to his aid and indicated the way
in which God would fulfil his counsel despite ap-
parent failure. He appropriated these state-
ments. He would fall now, but hereafter he
would come upon the clouds of heaven to hold
divine judgment and to establish an everlasting
kingdom. What a tremendous boldness! One
can hardly conceive a greater proof of the immediate and immovable certainty of the right-
ness and the worth of his cause. It is true that
this was not literally fulfilled, but it was fulfilled in a deeper and a truer sense. He came
not upon the clouds of heaven, he came in his
words, in his spirit, and in the historical effect
of the work of his life. The moment he died,
his Gospel was unexpectedly placed in freedom
and became indeed a great world-conquering
power. His cause proved itself to be the cause
of God and its enemies were reduced to an
echo, while it continued as an eternal and imperishable inheritance of humanity, bearing
within it the promise and the power of the whole
earth.

The catastrophe came. The Master's great
following might have caused it to linger a few
weeks longer, but the treachery of Judas has-
tened it. Jesus was condemned for blasphemy
by the Jewish Sanhedrim. The punishment,

according to Jewish law, was death, but it was not in their power to inflict it. He was therefore accused of insurrection before Pilate, his claim to the Messiahship being the pretext for it. Pilate must have known that the terms "Messiah" and "king of the Jews" had another significance from that set forth against the prisoner, and that he had to do with a "fanatic" and not with an enemy of the state. But the judge had other reasons for his course; he was undoubtedly anxious to placate Jewish feelings, which he had abundantly irritated. Jesus was made to undergo the punishment due to "treason," the punishment of the cross. Indeed the history of his suffering, even the great passion on Golgotha, had been lightly touched here and there by the legendary tendency. Traces of this are found in the following instances: the angel in the garden of Gethsemane, the healing of the ear of the servant of the high priest, the rending of the veil of the temple, the darkening of the sun, and the opening of the graves. But these blemishes can be very easily removed. And, after all deductions have been made, there remains the most sublime picture that history, the world artist, has ever painted; a picture so full of dramatic incident and single plastic scenes that there is hardly a pin-point, which—as Lessing said—has not commended itself to artistic effort; and what is still more, it is so rich in material for culture and elevation that the heart and the conscience are ever returning to it, with no sign of exhausting the source.

One will be inclined to close this history with Golgotha, thinking that, according to the historical and critical view, "the close as well as the commencement of the life of Jesus lay within the realm of the legendary, and that what is related concerning Golgotha is no longer history." Such a view would find support both in the tangible contradictions found in the narratives of the resurrection in the several Gospels and in the equally tangible growth and self-development of the legend from Mark to Matthew, to Luke, and to John. And yet this case is very different from that of the birth legends. We have no traces of them in the oldest parts of the narratives, their historicity is excluded by Paul and by the Gospels themselves, and these representations betray their own lateness. The exact opposite is true of the conviction that Jesus came forth from the dead. One may almost affirm that no fact in history is better attested than, not indeed the resurrection, but the firm conviction of the first Christian community of the resurrection of the Christ. Indeed, it is evident that the accounts of the Gospels themselves, even that of Mark, are legendary. But we have *one* account which is certainly one or more decades older than all the accounts of the Gospels, which criticism has not impugned and which narrates with almost mathematical accuracy the "manifestations" of Jesus. A contest had risen in Corinth respecting the fact of the resurrection. To quiet this, Paul* enumerates the several appearances of the risen Christ, giving the names of the witnesses, whom he in most cases knew and whom he declared yet alive, describing them with what was evidently the greatest care, order, and completeness. At the conclusion, he mentions himself and his own experience on the way to Damascus. Things look essentially different here from what they do in the subsequent Gospel narratives, being plainer and more moderate. We find nothing of the spectacular here, no trace of the angels and the accompanying phenomena, or of a call to the "open grave," or of a material resurrection. Paul evidently classes all "manifestations" with his own, namely, as a "vision," an inner experi-

* 1 Cor. 15, 5.

ence and perception of the living† Christ; an experience, however, that affords the most absolute certainty. This conviction was the firm reason for his entire ministry, his apostolate, and his whole spiritual existence. It was, undoubtedly, the united conviction of the first Christian community, and undoubtedly accounts for its origin and continuance. Without this conviction, the discipleship would have dissolved and become a mere echo; with it, they became heroes, apostles, martyrs, and created the Church. Historical criticism is certainly called upon to establish the fact of this certainty; no more and no less.

Was this conviction a self-delusion? Or did it, despite legendary and sensuous garnishments, rest, in the last analysis, upon a real fact? Historical criticism has nothing to say for or against life after death. The subject belongs to another realm. to the science of metaphysics and to the region of personal conviction. It is undoubtedly a special case under the most important question of all: "Does personality belong to the realm of the perishable? or does it belong to the realm of the eternal? Does

† An experience which we might illustrate if we had a clear conception of a ministry from will to will and from soul to soul, completing itself not in the customary way of the senses but immediately

death end all, or is it simply a passáge to higher existence?'' If it is the latter, criticism and historical science has nothing to oppose to the conviction of the disciples, that they know that their Lord had come forth from the dead. On the contrary, the circumstance that Jesus, who realized spiritual power to the full, both ethically and religiously—and all such as he,—had an experience that lifted him above the perishable,—this circumstance will always be the foundation for the conviction that the spirit has no share in the decay of the flesh. But these questions have no room here; they belong to an exhaustive treatment of the right and the necessity of an idealistic and religious view of the world in general.

THE TEACHINGS OF JESUS.

What did Jesus desire? What did he contribute to the world? To understand this, one must set aside all dogmatic and traditional schemes and investigate the subject in an absolutely historic spirit.

Jesus commenced his ministry with the announcement of the coming "kingdom," a subject which was quite familiar and which had already formed the bulk of the Baptist's ministry. He was far from making any new announcement. He knew nothing of a universal and general religion, nothing that might be termed the religion of humanity. His movement was local, temporary and of the most restricted character, proceeding from historical premises, a movement which can be understood only in the light of its own background; a movement which addressed itself to an unique situation. It was certainly not the eternal Gospel, it was a phase of religious culture which passed away

with the circumstances that gave it birth, the
significance of which was clearly pointed out
in the preceding chapter. Jesus was thoroughly
imbued with the religious faith of his time that
at last the long desired restoration of all things
was at hand. Descending from above, God was
about to shake the heavens and the earth. Old
things were to pass away. Everything was to
be completely changed, for now the kingdom of
God itself was to be realized on earth. At last
the protracted complaints which the righteous
and the God-fearing had raised from the days
of the Psalmist onward, the complaints, the im-
precations, and the curses against the destroyer
from without, the heathen and the kings of the
nations; as well as against the enemies of the
saints from within, the haughty, the powerful
and the courtly rich—all these were to be
hushed. God was to wipe away all tears, and
there was to be neither crying nor pain any
more. The mouth was to be full of laughter
and the tongue of boasting, when this kingdom
was to descend in its glory. This joyful message was the Gospel, the very Gospel which
Jesus himself preached literally at the beginning. And indeed his "Believe in the Gospel"
was at first no other than the old "Believe that
the kingdom of consolation is at hand." The
coming of this kingdom was redemption. To

enter into it was to be saved and to be blessed. Indeed "the hope of the kingdom," which was cherished by the pious and the silent in the land, was very different from the purely nationalistic idea. Its ideal was altogether "secularly" political. Its God was the God of a people of common descent, and its salvation a political act. The other ideal was definitely religious. It was the sore and peculiar trial of the spiritual people that the faithful and the pious were compelled to submit, on the one hand, to the heathen from without, and, on the other, to the godless from within; and the leading features of their salvation consisted in the attainment of freedom, justification by faith, and trust in God. But even then the kingdom hoped for was no abstraction, no mere subjective blessedness, no "kingdom of heaven" according to our understanding of the term; but a thoroughly external, local, and present thing, achieving external fortune, the golden Jerusalem, and the rule of the pious. Even Jesus shared these views,—shared, if you will, "the utopianism" of his age. He spoke of eating and drinking in the kingdom of God, and his disciples were to sit on twelve thrones "judging," that is, governing the twelve tribes of Israel, and ruling with him. Thus, he did not at first formally separate himself from the

Baptist; he seemed to have only the same call as he, namely, to be a Jewish preacher of repentance and—an "utopist."

Meanwhile we proceed at once to make some necessary qualifications: First, the very thing noticed about the preaching of the Baptist was true in a greater degree of Jesus. If any one would compare the preaching of Jesus with the phantasies and the "eschatological" ideas of his age, which have come down to us, he would see at once how remote he was from all of them. While entire books were devoted at that time to the discussion of the last things, the references of Jesus to them are scanty and meagre, and where these are to be found they hardly agree with one another. For instance, he spoke in one place of eating and drinking within the kingdom, implying a continuation of present conditions, whereas in another place he excludes them: "They will be like angels in heaven." He did not undertake to say "how" and "when" this kingdom was to come, a very feverish subject in that age. He knew neither the day nor the hour of its appearance and hardly mentions a thing concerning the content and conditions of this new kingdom; he was not interested in it for its own sake. All his interest centered immediately in the statement: "The kingdom is coming, therefore it behooves you to be ready." This was largely the case with John the Baptist. The announcement of the kingdom and its coming had already become a soul cure for him, a goal, so to speak, which carried with it the idea of a return to God, to piety and morality; and these were regarded at first as means conditioning the coming of the kingdom. But as soon as these were realized, they won a value of their own, and the emphasis passed over to them.

But the process thus began by John was carried to completion by Jesus. What was once regarded as only a condition to something else, became itself an end. Preaching of the religious and ethical type, planting of piety and righteousness, and the cure of souls became the proper calling and content of his life. He reversed the order of preaching. What before had been secondary now became primary, what before had been provisional now became final. Large portions of his preaching were given up to the removal of matter pertaining to the kingdom, matter which had no further general validity. And there was much else which was closely connected with the "preaching of the kingdom," but which, could be so removed as to inflict no injury upon the subject under discussion. Under the covering of the "preaching of the kingdom," he became the great curé and shepherd of his people and of his community, planting a spiritual life, that is, an inwardness possessing absolutely peculiar worth.

"An inwardness possessing absolutely peculiar worth"—this is our second point, and it needs careful comment as the more essential thing. In comparison with the "preaching of the kingdom." the religious and ethical phases now receive the emphasis and pass into the foreground; and not only that, but the preaching becomes something entirely different from, something incomparably higher than, that of his predecessors. It planted dispositions and ideals and created a piety and morality with which even a John was not acquainted. This gave him precedence over all his forerunners. The view that the kingdom was at hand, and that therefore repentance was needed, he shared with the Baptist and with others. This was not his new contribution, but was a perishable inheritance with which his generation had provided him, and it made him only a pious Jew of the first century. It was the new piety which he awoke and the new righteousness which he demanded that made him Jesus, the light of the world.

Jesus certainly demanded that they "do the will of God." But this was nothing new, this was an old demand. But what had hitherto been

regarded as "the will of God"? The law, the
thora. Now this law had the most diversified
contents: precepts of a social character, of
right, and of divine service, ceremonies and observances, especially precepts respecting "purity," particularly ritual and Levitical purity,
respecting abstinence from all kinds of food,
contacts, stains, washings, and expiatory customs and the like. Embedded among all of these
were also commands of a purely religious and
ethical character which referred not to external
things but to the conscience; for instance, the
"ten commandments" or such a demand as,
"Thou shalt love thy neighbor as thyself." But
these were not properly appreciated, because
they mingled indiscriminately with ceremonial
and ritual precepts. The duty of loving one's
brother was placed along side of ritual observances as if they were of equal worth. And it
was worse even that that; where ethical and
ceremonial duties clashed, the former had to
give way. Men watched with greater anxiety
for the exact form of some sacrificial obliga-
tions than for love to their fellows, for ritual
purity than for purity of heart. The first act
of Jesus was to emancipate the ethical. He
freed it from that dangerous conjunction and
conformation with the ceremonial, the ritual,
and the legal. He discerned its unique worth,

and set it apart. He did not at first contend polemically against the ceremonial and the ritual. He did not forbid the further consideration of it. He even obeyed it as a whole himself. But he expressed his opinion of it clearly in condemning the man who deemed it more important to fulfil his sacrificial duty than his parental duty; in his doctrine of the Sabbath when he taught, "The Sabbath was made for man, and not man for the Sabbath"; in his reference to the Levitical law and all the anxious observances and cleansing of vessels connected with it, when he said, "Not that which goeth into the mouth defileth a man, but that which cometh out of the mouth." The clearest statement of all was when he spoke of love to God and to one's neighbor in the words: "On these two commandments hang all the law and the prophets." Drawing this line of distinction clearly between the ritual sphere and the ethical sphere, he was able to show to the conscience what was the "will of God" and what was not, and to lead for the first time the ethical consciousness to its purity. It was this in particular that led to his destruction, and that, to the adherents of the existing conditions, was the most obtrusive and dangerous of his innovations; yet it had only a secondary relation to his deepest and most characteristic message.

The new message in religion, of which Jesus himself was conscious when he said that John was the greatest born of woman, but that the least in the kingdom of heaven was greater than he, and which was to divide the old from the new, Christ from his predecessors, was something still higher.

What was this new and still higher thing? It was something of extraordinary simplicity, something that did not call for many words, and yet it was something very great. It could not be characterized as a new "knowledge of God," or a profound all-embracing theology, or a new theoretic conception of the relation of the Godhead to the world, or of the infinite ground of things to its phenomena and its effects, or of the eternal to the temporal, or of the present to that which lies beyond. As a matter of fact he cherished the naive, anthropomorphic conception of things, which simple, Judaic theism had previously developed: God as a king enthroned in heaven, looking down upon things and ruling the world with his omnipotent power. He did not bring a new theology but a new piety; not a new theoretic conception of eternity, but a new practical conduct and disposition toward it. We may say that he was the first to bring, in a general way, true piety into the world. God had, indeed, been real enough to Judaism, but only indirectly and through His law. He was respected as the defender of the law, but there was no real and vital relation to Him, no lasting and experiential possession of Him in mind and in spirit. This was the very thing that Jesus brought in and made vital. Henceforth piety consisted not in obedience to law and the expectation of reward and punishment from its mighty Preserver and Executor; these now became a matter of indifference. Piety, in the future, meant to possess God and His presence at all times in an experiential way, that is, to fill the entire life with the feeling of His nearness. And this feeling was not one of fear and overwhelming horror in the presence of the supernatural, as heretofore in the Old Testament and in all heathen religions; it was a feeling of the deepest reverence and meekness in the presence of Him, who sits enthroned above all the world and all creatures in unspeakable secrecy, the name of whom is Holiness. At the same time it contained a liberating, redeeming, and childlike trust which lifted its possessor above all servitude into eternal love, a trust which knew all existence, even its own, even single and little things, firmly infolded in the eternal care and providence, and which did not permit itself to be led astray by tribulation, exercising the childlike spirit even in Gethsemane. This was the spirit that prayed, "Not as I will, but as thou wilt." This was not a superficial optimism, which closed its eyes to the hardness, the difficulty, and the enigma of life. Jesus saw and suffered it all. It was rather a courageous and resolute idealism which, in spite of all opposition, mystery, and death, continued to believe in eternal love as the last meaning and intention of things. There was indeed nothing superficial and weak in this faith in the divine "Fatherhood." For here God was regarded pre-eminently as the representative and essence of the moral law, which pledges one to absolute honesty and truth. To call this God "Father" was to submit one's self completely to the ethical order of the world and to do it regardless of consequences. "Be ye perfect, even as your Father which is in heaven is perfect." This new piety made itself known in many sayings and parables; but the simplest way of expressing it was by the term "Father" and its correlate "sons of God" for the disciples of Jesus; and its creed was the Lord's prayer.

This new religion, which was the religion of Jesus, was not the product of reflection or thought, of speculation or philosophic endeavor, or of any kind of demonstration. It was the spontaneous result of his religious and genial individuality, a veritable spring issuing from depths that no scientific, psychological analyses could fathom or laws of development explain. Jesus presented it not as a novelty or a thing of wonder, but as the natural and proper thing for him to do. It issued from the depths of his own life freely and easily that it might also become the property of others, yet it was considered for a long time as a novelty. It was his deepest life and he gave it gladly. Because he had experienced God within his own life, because he had realized the divine Sonship within himself, because he knew that he was Son and that God was his Father, those who would partake of his fulness might receive the same blessing. This he had discerned himself; and in one of the great moments of his life, this knowledge broke forth joyfully in the words, ''No one knows the Son save the Father, neither knoweth any man the Father, save the Son, and he to whomsoever the Son will reveal him.''

This was the message of Jesus. It was no imperfect or provisional message, it was the perfect redemption. Wherever it entered, all slavish fear, all servility, all anxiety, all pinching care was driven away. This piety was itself the best redemption. It rooted the mind in freedom. The eternal world was brought into

the midst of life as a subject of experience and
even of possession; it penetrated with its light
and its warmth into the hearts of men. Life
was lifted to a new and altogether different
plane, and received a tremendous impulse. Man
awoke to the consciousness of his eternal worth.
And this piety was not for a class, not for ex-
ceptionally gifted characters, as past forms of
piety had been, it was possible for every one,
who had a longing for the living God.

But this "new righteousness"—to return
once more to the subject—grew in this high
region into the full broad ideal of Jesus. We
saw above how he freed the ethical from false
connections and entanglements; we must now
add that he, at the same time, deepened it in-
finitely, placing it upon the right basis and giving it new content. Furthermore, he made
known the necessary and indeed the only connection that one needs to affirm between "religion" and "morality," that wherever the
eternal world is a real and vital part of human
life, it has also breadth and depth enough to
include the ethical; more than this, it is prepared to perceive the ethical itself as eternal,
absolute, and plainly obligatory. In the soil
of this new piety, the ethical perception and
judgments of Jesus gained of necessity an energy and a tension the like of which they had

never hitherto attained, either in Judaistic or
Grecian life and thought. The doing of the good
is not a mercantile transaction; it must possess
the whole man; it must be seized and accomplished with iron resolution. "If thy right eye
offend thee pluck it out and cast it from thee."
The parables of The Treasure Hid in a
Field and The Pearl of Great Price, which
inculcate the principle of hazarding all to gain
"the one thing necessary," have a like import.
This was not rigorism, not scrupulous petti-
ness, not squeamishness of conscience about individual things. Jesus' ideal of righteousness
was completely free from all this. His ideal
was large-featured, simple, standing in complete contrast to all miserable calculations and
merchandizing as well as to all self-inflicted cas-
uistry and pettifoggery, which had hitherto
been practised. No other course was possible
to one who was so full of the absolute obliga-
tion of the moral law and of the highest con-
centrated moral energy and determination.
Thus it was that he at once awoke, purified, and
deepened the sense of sin and guilt.

The preaching of Jesus was never guilty of
cant about the "tendency to sin," which ends
mostly in frittering away the sense of guilt. On
the contrary, the issue is met with deep earnest-
ness. To miss the point was not an error, not

an oversight traceable to the reason, not a misfortune due to environment and natural disposition, nor indeed mere pollution, defilement, and contact with the ugly and the commonplace, which the esthetic sense could not complacently endure. But it was sin, and as such it was "the greatest evil," not because of its evil consequences, but because of its denial of the highest nobility of the human soul and because of its severing of the connection between it and God. The preaching of Jesus showed the true and only way to remove guilt, not by any external manipulations, such as washings, consecrations, and acts of atonement, set forth and recommended by Judaism and Grecianism; but by the way set forth in the parables of the Prodigal Son and The Lost Sheep, the way of deep and genuine repentance. Furthermore, Jesus placed righteousness where it belonged, in the disposition and the heart; not in the deed or the word, not in the hand or the mouth. There is nothing good in this world, but "the good will." The man must be good at the center, else his words and his deeds are not good, and if he is good at heart, all care for the externals of life is vain and unnecessary. For the will is inwardly identified with its ideal, and the ethical action proceeds for the first time freely and without constraint and is consequently genuine and full of worth; "a good tree cannot bring forth evil fruit, neither can a corrupt tree bring forth good fruit." Hence the ethical deed is no longer an isolated thing, no longer a numerical magnitude, no longer a thing of weight and measurement, nor does it admit of more or less or of a surplus. One cannot do more than his duty. The workers who began in the morning, could do no more than they who began at the eleventh hour; they all could but do their duty, and God gave alike to them. And since there is no reckoning nor measuring, one cannot reckon or measure beforehand to demand a recompense from God. "When ye shall have done all those things which are commanded you, say, We are unprofitable servants; we have done that which it was our duty to do."

And thus it proceeded. Views and knowledges of the profoundest character sprang up everywhere; views which passed long ago into the general consciousness becoming the classical and fundamental rules for all high and genuine morality, and which broadened out into an astonishing fulness of individual traits, into unforgetable formulations and expressions, pregnant with a multitude of fine observations respecting human kind and humanity. But these views culminated in their pronouncement upon personality and its transcendent worth as compared with all earthly goods: "What profiteth a man, if he gain the whole world and lose his own soul?" Indeed Greek philosophy had already been a culture of the inner man and a cure of the soul. But here the cure of the soul was the whole thing; it was its salvation. The question of the religious and ethical content of the life of the soul became central, before which all others vanished; it was a question of life and death. Now this led necessarily to that which we call "personality" and "individuality." The new piety and its fundamental thought of divine sonship made for this. Grecian morality had lifted up a high ethical ideal of human life and dignity, but it was "impersonal" in a peculiar sense. It had set up the rational, the thought element, the logical side of our nature as constituting the truly human in man. But this is not that which constitutes "personality." When we speak of personality, we think of character, and the matter that goes to the making of character does not proceed from the cognitive and intellectual faculties, but from the will, the disposition, and the affection. And this is the very side of the man that the Gospel seeks to develop. The trust, the reverence, the meekness and the love which it demands are affections and acts that emanate from the will. Its fundamental trait is thoroughly dispositional not intellectual. On the contrary, Grecian ethics and thought emphasize the general, the typical, the "idea," not the individual, and, in turn, the reason, the rational as it is alike in all men. But the Gospel emphasizes the person. It is not man's rationality that constitutes him the "child of God" and the object of the divine love, but his person, his "isolated personality."

If we now study the content of this "new righteousness" of Jesus, it is in general plain morality, attested by the conscience and partly contained already in the prophetic preaching of the Old Testament. But it was Jesus who disclosed its full meaning by his "highest command" of pure neighbor love. Even the ancient covenant contained this: "Thou shalt love thy neighbor as thyself." But it was one commandment among many. Christ drew it forth placing it and love to God in the first place, making it the fundamental law of his fellowship and the distinguishing mark of those who seriously attached themselves to him. In the Old Testament, brotherhood is limited to the line of descent and nationality; in the New Testament, Jesus makes it as wide as the need of man, including even one's enemies and illustrating the same by the parable of the good Samaritan. The highest proof of such love is to love one's enemy. But this love is not a characterless, indolent sufferance of all things, not an apathy towards any and all evil, or Jesus would have but poorly illustrated it; it is not that, but it is the strong virtue that can love the neighbor in the enemy, pray for those who despitefully use us and bless those who curse us. This and compassion that knows no conditions, pardon even to the "seventy times seven," overcoming of evil with good, and love to the lost are the five great proofs of the love of one's neighbor demanded by Jesus. And these are completely misunderstood, if one interprets them as a weak, effeminate set of qualities or as a cloak covering mere "good nature." One must regard all five as thoroughly surcharged with the fundamental disposition of the Gospel of Jesus. And each of these is wholly degenerate, unless it is the vigorous product of the ethical will. One understands this thoroughly and at once if he attempts to think of Jesus himself or one of his most genuine followers, say Paul or Augustine or Luther as merely "good natured." Further, the ethical ideal of the "new righteousness" magnifies itself in all the known demands of purity of heart, sincerity, truthfulness without the oath and the like, and has woven for itself a garland of peculiar dispositions, not lending themselves readily to statutes and paragraphs but winning for the whole, for the first time, the ring of genuineness; for instance, the disposition of absolute meekness towards God and that of absolute independence towards men, the forbidding of anxious care as a heathen sin substituting for it the bright joyous conception of life, which stands in such rugged opposition to that of John the Baptist and which has something of pleasure in it "whiling away sweet life," the piety which permeates everything and accompanies but does not identify itself with mystical secrecy and separatism, and particularly the command, "Be as little children." This last characterizes the message of Jesus as no other does. It shows a complete contrast to all the religious technicalities, artificialities and perversities of the age, and, at the same time, his simplicity, his immediateness and candor in everything, in faith, action and conduct of life. This is the most secret, the most difficult and the finest thing in all Christendom, a condition which is in the religious realm what genius is in the artistic realm, a condition where the categoric imperative and all forms of physical force are left far behind and where faith and ethical action spring up spontaneously and abundantly, a condition where all mechanical activities avail not, be-

cause of the call for a deep and a self-sacrific-
ing spirit, a condition to be attained only by
the completest change in thought and will. This
was called later "the new birth," than which
no more pregnant a figure could be found.

This was the preaching and the ministry of
Jesus. Its center and well-spring was the new
piety, the consciousness of the divine sonship,
of union with God, and this as a restful, permanent, and blessed possession of life. In this
union with God was given at once the strong
foundation and the constant source of supply
for its free, pure, and deep morality. With
these two he certainly brought an "Eternal
Gospel," not merely to his own people, but to
the people of the world. It is true however
that many a problem was solved only tem-
porarily in his presentation of the new righteousness and that it was not a complete code for
all questions and for all time. But in its great
ruling thoughts was provided the permanent
foundation for the true human ethics. And our
great metaphysical problems, the relation of the
eternal to the temporal, of the Here to the Beyond, and of the infinite to the finite have
greatly changed from what they were in primitive ages; they have grown and have assumed
other proportions. Our representations of God
no longer fit into the homely imagery of the

heavenly king upon an invisible throne. We know that this is only a figurative expression, as is all our talk about Him. The theology and the philosophy of our age are striving after new expressions to grasp that eternal and other-world reality, that eternal governing Power, which lies at the base of the actual world. But wherever this highest ruling Power is grasped and understood as a Holy Will, encompassing with infinite power the greatest and the least and directing them according to eternal ends, and wherever a person submits himself to it in meekness and in absolute trust and thus wins strength, freshness and joy for the conduct of such an ideal life, there one finds a disciple of Jesus. Such a person is what the Master would expect today of his disciple. He would then be what the disciples were.

If we now glance backward for a moment at the above mentioned relations of the most essential elements in the history of Jesus to the announcement of the "approaching kingdom," it has become clear how completely this preaching and its ideals had outgrown the character of being merely provisional or preparatory; they could no longer be thrust back into the old frame-work. The coming kingdom had no longer any surprises for one so "prepared." The thousand clusters of grapes, which were to grow

on one tendril, the fruitfulness of the fields
and all the other treasures, which were expected, must be grandly indifferent to him who
had meanwhile entered into the disposition, the
feeling, and the ideals with which the preaching
of Jesus had already completely filled the heart.
This indeed explains the indifference of Jesus
to the peculiar contents of the coming kingdom;
an indifference that never attempted to picture
its coming glory and that passed by the phantasies of its age respecting the last things. But
more than this, he was strongly possessed of
the thought that in his ministry and spiritual
deliverances he had brought the long-expected
redemption. This thought had not become absolutely clear to him, gaining for itself formu-
lated expression, but it was present and left
traces of itself. His entire ministry was without that impatient expectation so characteristic
of John. On the contrary, it was pervaded by
a sense of the most blessed possession. The
merchant found his costly pearl, and the treas-
ure-digger, his treasure. What more could they
desire? Meanwhile the consciousness could
grow within him that in his preaching was fulfilled the prophecy that righteous men and
prophets had been expecting: ''Many prophets
and righteous men desired to see what you see,
and have not seen it, and to hear what you hear

and have not heard it." And it is noticeable enough and intelligible that, even with Jesus, the customary meaning of the "kingdom of God" was being modified, and was losing its exclusively temporal character. It no longer designated an inheritance yet to come, but it was silently being transformed into an entirely new significance, into that of an internal condition, an internal possession, a fortune already possessed, a rule of God already active, a community of equals, redeemed and God-serving, already present. This new significance of the word in Jesus was by no means a completed fact; but its presence was powerfully felt.] See especially his parables on the kingdom of heaven, particularly that wondrously deep one of Mark iv. 26: The kingdom of heaven is as if a man cast seed into the ground. Then he departs. Forthwith it grows without any assistance, silently and imperceptibly, without compulsion, without rule, without pressure, and without any artificial activity, but spontaneously as the corn, first the blade, then the ear, and then the full corn in the ear. What springs up thus is not that external kingdom which comes like lightning, but which is not sown and does not grow. On the contrary, it is the still, silent growth and development of the inner man, which knows nothing of compulsion and rule, but which advances according to its own nature, just as the corn that drops into prepared soil. The same thing is taught by the mustard seed parable, Mark iv. 30. It is not the "kingdom of heaven" that comes suddenly from above and that pertains to temporalities that grows and extends itself; it is the ministry of the announcement of Jesus. This grows from insignificant beginnings into a great tree, and we shelter today under its branches. Likewise in Luke, xvi. 16: "The law and the prophets were until John; since that time the kingdom of God is preached and every man presseth into it." The joyful message here is no longer as elsewhere, that of the coming kingdom. The message of the coming kingdom was more direct and much more energetic in John. The message of Jesus referred to present salvation, the salvation of divine sonship. This is evident from the statement: "Every one presseth into it." Now no man could force himself into the kingdom that was to come suddenly. One could only wait in patience until God willed to reveal it. And, finally, we refer to the episode of Luke, xvii. 20: Being questioned by the pharisees, when the kingdom of God was to come, he answered them, saying: "The kingdom of God cometh not with observation. They will not say, lo here or lo there, because behold the kingdom of God is within you." One indeed observes the paradoxical character of this as yet unusual statement; but the new representation is indeed completely at hand. And Paul's interpretation and setting forth of it is quite accurate, Rom. xiv. 17: "The kingdom of God is righteousness, joy and peace in the Holy Ghost."

But in conclusion we must guard ourselves from a fundamental misapprehension of the Gospel of Jesus. It has often been regarded as an escape from the world and the sorrows of the world, a kind of ascetic and cloistral ideal of life. People object to this idea of it, because of its indifference to gain and possession, to national, political, and social tasks and to many other things, which many of us deem the highest and noblest interests of life; and they do so apparently with justice. And on the other hand, objection is made to such apparently dark and fanatical demands as, "If thy right hand offend thee, cut it off," etc.

But let us begin with this second point. These demands are not at all fanatical, are not even "ascetic" in the true sense of that word, but simply intelligible. These are demands that every idealism, every intelligible idealism, emphasizes and must emphasize. Wherever a man submits himself to his ideals, he does so entirely, soul and body, for they do not permit compromise at all; this must be so or else they are no ideals. They imply renunciations and sacrifices under the hardest conditions, and conflicts of the bitterest kind; but these are all necessary. This is always true when the questions of ideals or of conscience are uppermost; resignation to God and submission to the moral law. It was the greatness of Jesus to embody the demand of the ideal in decisive and complete one-sidedness, and to cause it to stand forth not only as a demand but as a finished product, incomparably magnificent and completely unique, confirmed both in life and in death.

But the former objections are conceded to prove nothing for the ostensibly negative character of the ethics of Jesus. Indeed the question does not treat of any inner aversion of the Christian principle itself to the subjects in discussion. But if the belief that the end of things is at hand continues to burden people it is naturally impossible to expect the growth and the development of any intelligently new political and social interests and ideals. Further, consider this: the particular mission of Jesus is within the sphere of the religious and the ethical. But the idea of a call to anything implies that the whole life should be wholly and intelligently devoted to the prosecution of only one

end. The more a person realizes himself to be
called for a special purpose, the more will this
consciousness grow within him. Jesus' knowledge of his calling is clearly indicated in Luke,
xii. 14: "Man, who made me a judge and a di-
vider over you?" Likewise, it is the same consciousness of the necessary one-sidedness of
his calling that speaks in his answer to the
Syro-Phoenician woman, "I am not sent but
unto the lost sheep of the house of Israel."

Furthermore, to conceive Jesus as an ascetic
is to profoundly misunderstand his character,
his piety, and his temper. One can hardly make
a greater mistake. This is indeed the opposite
of the truth, for in this lay his greatest difference from the Baptist. We find John in the
wilderness; we find Jesus among men, entering
into their joys, their feasts, their companion-
ships and struggles. The preaching of John
was sad, gloomy, and heavy; the preaching of
Jesus was full of light and glory. John's disposition was that of a slave; the disposition of
Jesus and his followers was that of the free-
born sons of God. The faith of John was that
of the Old Testament type, harsh and full of
fear; the faith of Jesus that of triumphant and
childlike certainty, dwelling beyond all fear and
care. John commanded fasts; Jesus forbade
them. John was an exemplary ascetic, wearing

the hairy mantle, living the hermit life, and eating locusts and wild honey. Jesus knew nothing of all this; no peculiar repentance, no spiritual methods and rules of order; he dissolved
all observances, founding only the God-inspired
disposition, which was to issue freely in the
choice of the good. John exemplified the ascetic
and the monkish type of piety; Jesus was the
opposite of this and he knew this full well. Here
are his own words: "No man seweth a new piece
of cloth on an old garment—And no man put-
teth new wine into old bottles," etc. Mark, ii.
22. This was his meaning when he permitted
himself to be deprecatingly called a glutton, a
winebibber, and a friend of publicans and sinners, and when he answered the surprising
question of John's disciples as to why his disciples did not fast, saying, "Can the companions of the bridechamber mourn as long as the
bridegroom is with them?"

No piety is so remote from the monkish and
cloistral type of religion as that of Jesus, so
alien to the activities peculiar to that class of
institutions. Mystical dispositions and ecstatic
joy may be taught and fostered in such places,
but not the piety of Jesus. His piety calls at
once for life, for many kinds of experience, for
the world of men, for fortune, for the cross, and
for the entire play of life, in order to become

the eternal ground tone of it all. It can be as little separated from the complexities of life and continue to thrive as a melody from its variations. The same thing is true of its new righteousness as of its piety. The old righteousness of the pharisees was thoroughly "ascetic"; it was the leaven that was to be swept away. The plain morality of Jesus does not admit of any ascetic additions. Its content is plain duty, which also presupposes the world, brethren and communion with them. The fundamental command is, love. This cuts away the roots from asceticism in all its forms. The monk, the fugitive from the world, can love no neighbor; indeed he has none. Love presses immediately into life, and works with and for men. So let one conceive that small portion of the Scripture which speaks of the impending end of the world, taken away from the Gospel; let one conceive the joyful, courageous disposition of Jesus which contemplates the world, the strong ethical will, and especially this love to man and to all that is human to be freed from its small narrow self-enclosed communities and to be placed face to face with multifarious life and its tasks, and it will be seen to enter into it as into its own most peculiar sphere. Apart from this sphere, the Gospel becomes stunted and dry.

The above objections and others which might
be mentioned do not present themselves when
the sermons of Jesus are interpreted, as they
should be, in the light of his image and character. The traditional view strives to derive itself from the character of Jesus. It represents
him either as that dogmatic "double-being,"
that "compound person," of whom no man can
properly affirm character, or as the incorpora-
tion of "the man-in-himself," that is, universal humanity in a person. Both conceptions
fail when we compare them with the image that
the Gospel narrative presents to us. This image
is no universal concept, no mere abstraction in
a person. It steps forth with decisive individuality, with utmost naturalness and with well-de-
fined character. And what an image! To see
it clearly we must turn aside all dogmatic and
half-dogmatic delineations, all those images
small and great, which come to us from a false
artistic tradition; as those of Hoffman, Thu-
mann and Gabriel Max, where the heads are
soft, mild and almost effeminately sweet, the
hair closely parted and waving, with or without
those fanatical eye-lashes and the somewhat
enervated, consumptive, repentant, and ascetic
form, the lines of the face partly good-natured
and partly fanatical. These pictures have been
made to follow all kinds of artistic or inartistic

and phantastic ideals, but not the historic image of the first three Gospels. No one would divine from these that he called two of his disciples "sons of thunder" and that these two belonged to the inner circle of the disciples; that he rebukingly said to Peter "get thee behind me Satan, for thou art an hindrance to me"; that he dubbed his enemies "whited sepulchers full of all uncleanness"; that he took a whip of small cords to clean the temple of the money changers; that with splendid scorn he denominated Herod, "the fox"; that he could return thanks to the heavenly Father; and that he could fight with his own heart in the hottest battle and in the bitterest sorrow. One would never divine from these that highest natural temperament, which formed the basis of the character of the Christ. Add to this natural temperament, the religious and ethical consciousness that was his, and we are face to face with the most wonderful character. This temperament possesses the incomparable strength of the ethical will, the passion for depth and fervor, the glow and the dauntless energy, which come from resignation to God, to one's calling, and to one's brethren. He possessed such an inner concentration, such an hierarchy of powers, such a consciousness of self and of God as were able to carry him victoriously through all the storms of life. Hence he had an inner certainty, a deep assurance, which profited in every condition and which made the plain Nazarene, the carpenter's son, superior to all the scribes, the high priests, and the Roman Procurator. He was an upright, resplendent, genuine, free-born and truly kingly being. But he also possessed and manifested—as if he dared not to fail in anything—the warmest feeling and the purest love. Where all failed he knew how to understand, to pardon, to raise up, and to console. Publicans and sinners whom others cast out, he sought, discovered and awakened the flickering spark of their faith and love. He made friends of the children and commended the childlike disposition to the disciples as a pattern and as an entrance into the kingdom of heaven. But over and above all this extended the naturalness, the sweetness, the freshness, the glory and the charm of his being and especially of his words, the multifarious and transparent quality of his thought and images, the plasticity of his parables, and the inexhaustible and many-sided character of the world of his ideas. These sprang up and flowed forth so easily, so lightly, so full of intelligence and spontaneity as to become at once classical and imperishable; without being pathetic and solemn, with everything that was highest and best, this teaching was comprehensible to the plainest man and, at the same time, full of infinite matter to the deepest.

And we have this all indeed only in fragments, in pieces, falsely put together by the unskillfulness of tradition; we see it all, so to speak, in a dark and badly broken mirror! What must this have been to those who heard him with their own ears, and had an experience of him! What must the original have been, if the disfigured image is so resplendent! Truly the historical image loses none of the reverence, which the disciples of Jesus brought at all times to the Master. Indeed it does not lead us back to the old pictures with the Jesus lamb, or to the sentimental forms of the earliest Jesus of the mystics; but it leads us by so much the more to a fundamental and ever growing "heroworship," which breaks out anew with freshness and joy into the ancient acclaims and confessions: *Christ our Lord, our Hero, our King.* And it is a matter of disposition and individual thought what form this reverence is to take and what depth it is to attain.

A CLOSING WORD.

So much in answer to the question as to the life of Jesus historically conceived. A number of other questions now follow. What significance has the preaching of Jesus for us, for our convictions, and for our faith and our endeavor after piety. What significance has his person to the validity of his preaching? For it is already evident that for such an announcement as his, its claim for truth and absolute validity, the person of the announcer has much more significance than that of Euclid for the validity of his geometry. Further, there is the general question: Are the great phenomena and contents of the history to be conceived as a "revelation," announcing the way to know and to realize the eternal meaning and purpose of present day life? And suggested by this general question is the special one: Are we to regard the history of religion and especially the Israelitish religion and the phenomenon of Jesus as a "revelation"? And many like questions offer themselves. Opportunity may perhaps present itself to return to these questions. But it was necessary first of all to consider the more fundamental one. To repeat it once more: this was the chief aim, the aim that justifies these lectures.